Elicia Moore ~ La Uni Ca

Elicia Moore

BookLeaf
Publishing

Elicia Moore ~ La Uni Ca © 2023 Elicia
Moore

Presentation by *BookLeaf Publishing*

Web: www.bookleafpub.com

E-mail: info@bookleafpub.com

ISBN: 9789357740258

First edition 2023

From the book 'Sis, Don't Settle' by Faith Jenkins, I dedicate this book to my high-value self. I am "so invested in my personal development and growth that I have no time for drama, gossip, or any habits that don't move me forward toward greatness."

ACKNOWLEDGEMENT

This book came as no easy feat. I doubted myself at almost every turn but made it a point to tell the people closest in my life to help me stay accountable. Thank you God for blessing me with this gift and opportunity. It is in you that I live, move and have my being. To my true sisters, Sheena Love and Leah Martin. You've been listening to my poetry, snapping and encouraging me to step out and show the world what you both have always seen in me. You kept it real with me and you never allowed me to settle! I love how you love me! To my OG military sisters Doretha Samuels, Shawntel Carpenter and Danielle Hodo, I met you all during some of the most trying times of my life. Each in your own way showed me how to navigate this thing called life by rallying around me and often times be in the thick of it with me. I'm forever grateful for your lovingkindness and friendship. To my love sister, Tara McKnight, you gave me one of the greatest gifts I didn't know I needed - your mom! I love me some Mama Zola!! I met you during a major crossroad in my life. You were the first person to ever walk into my job, walk past my boss with no hesitation, sit down like you were an employee and make me take time to celebrate my accomplishments by planning my first vacation. You showed me the importance of celebrating me no matter how big or small. To my larger-than-life sister, Terryann Miller-Salter, I am not letting my baby die! You have been speaking into my life, showing up for me in ways unimaginable and holding me accountable since the beginning of this newfound creative journey. Thank you for putting me in positions that made me show up and step out. To my bona fide sister, Melisha Folk you taught me that I have the right to unapologetically show up for myself. Your charisma, fashion sense and don't take no mess attitude pushed me to fight for me even when you didn't realize you were doing it. To my trail blazing sisters Jas Rosales and Charlotte Lang who jumped right on my vision and had me behind a lens bringing it to life. Your compassion and genuineness to see others thrive right alongside you is a gift in itself! To my big sisters, Aisha Loveless and Harriett Braxton-Washington, through you I found a sisterhood in my creative element, an unapologetic love and opportunities I wouldn't have thought to be possible! Thank you for showing up for me even when you didn't know I was fighting to show up for myself! Always and forever rooting for you! To my tribe: Kim

Darby, Melody Sandiford, Cynthia Johnson, Kelly Green and Shelia Hearn, words are not enough to express how grateful I am for each of you, how much I love you and how extremely blessed I am to have each of you in my life and finally have a tribe I can call my own. To my true brother, Jerome Perry. I pray that you continue to be unimpressed by me because mediocracy is not acceptable. I love you to life! This book would not be if it wasn't for each and every one of you!

Anxiety

Why are you so loud
Wrecking my thoughts like you're white girl
wasted
Polluting my mind, sending my heart racing
I'm jumpin at every turn because my
surroundings don't feel familiar
The pressure is intense it' reached is maximum
capacity
I'm about to blow if I don't release this
monstrosity
Scared to even say something because it looks a
lot like guilt and regret
Hell, I don't have it together
Falling apart to get put back together???
God spare me the moment when the choice is
not but, either, or or
My voice so low because speaking normal it just
may crack and reveal my truth
I fight when I don't want to
I fight when it's hard to
I fight when I don't have to and
If I'm not careful, I'll fight you too
Music hard and ratchet so I can't hear my
thoughts
Screeching halt to my brain then I turn it all off

And I sit in silence as I call on my thoughts one at a time, raise your hand before you speak, don't talk at once

BECAUSE I CAN'T HEAR YOU LET ALONE MYSELF PLEASE SHUT THE HELL UP!!!

Don't worry, I'm grounding 3 things I can see, feel and hear
The song is in my head "Ain't no stopping sunshine, ain't no stopping me"
The affirmations on rotation "you are amazing, beautiful inside and out, you got this girl, you are a rockstar
But at any moment now, the tears will flow down my face, a rush of pressure will slowly seep into the crevices of my space
And because I won't turn the knob to release the pressure faster
I spend my day in agony saying "My life still matters"

Atelophobia 'The Fear Of Not Being Good Enough'

I got it tatted on my ribs so when I'm naked, I'll
remember
When I feel unprotected from the winding of my
mental gears
When someone says it's not you, it's me
When my priority level seems low and it seems
the world is fighting against me
Because I held my head down for so long and all
I can see is me
When I feel like I'm being swallowed alive
When the aching in my chest moves to the
Shaking in my hands and the tears running down
my face
When I'm sitting by myself trying to remind
myself that my life is a gift and I have a duty to
live
My best life being myself
When my spirit feels crushed by my fears
When there are more tears than ears
When there are more issues than tissue
Your fears are yelling to dismiss you
Some say forget everything and run while others
say face everything and rise.

I'll try to remember that I am the apple of God's
eye
Beyond what I can see
Before I knew what I felt had a name
He thought I was to die for and he's impressed
by me just the same
Sweet, beautiful woman that you are
Always know it's not how you feel
For it is He who created you to be, fearless and
unafraid
Don't discount God's good work He did in
creating you
You're good enough, you are more than enough
Heck, it is absolutely ridiculous how enough you
are
Don't give others the power to alter how you
view you
Lower your expectations of them and elevate
yourself higher
Level up above fear
Above life itself
Until you can't see your feet because they're
covered in the clouds
And when you create the space in your world
where you are the head, the Queen, the
Dutchess, the Empress and the Princess
Remember you are worth it
Courage comes after you do something you fear
so lift off and face it

Fear is your facade and greatness is your reality
The one you feed will be the one you see
So let your fight be stronger than your fear
You're better than you let on
Allow it to transcend
Showing all your true beauty and elegance
within
Atelophobia has no rule or reign
It's in your DNA to be…FEARLESS

Rule

There's a trigger
Sometimes I can plan for it
Contingency is preperation so I'm ready for it
But this time the trigger was pulled
Cocked back like shot gun
Unleashed like a machine gun
Held with ease like a hand gun
And I was so stunned I couldn't run
No time for cover, contingency or concealment
The world is about to witness
Just how anxiety rules my body and it's
unforgiving
I explode, bursting into tears
It felt like I was thrown in the ocean
Restricted from any motion
The current gets stronger
My breathing gets shallower and if I didn't
scream soon
My life wouldn't matter
JUST SPEAK UP I yell angrily to myself
Opening up the floodgates exposing
To all who are in close distance a glimpse of
what it feels like to be trapped by ANXIETY

Emptying myself I couldn't go back from what I
felt because although I released I'm still failing,
falling, drowning, crowning

The next day the pressure was so intense
My cry was relentless
No sniffling, or dramatics
But a steady flow of tears
Going at a steady pace like a summer's rain
Fear and pain flooding my brain
And it took every ounce of fight in me to gain
An ounce of dignity, an inch of tranquility
A moment of peace but it's still lingering
It's not always like this, just keep fighting
You can do this, just keep trying
This doesn't rule you there's no denying
But it's not always true because I can't stop
crying
Wired weird and funky I just want to end this
No one volunteers to feel hopeless yet my hand
is up screaming yes
My heart says stay open and exposed
You have to feel
This can't rule you
You plan so you can heal
My mind says girl you must be tripping you
haven't learned from the last
Shut it down, stay in control that's the way your
body goes

Snatched back into reality just when I think it's
over
My body is thrown back in the ocean where it all
begins
Current rushing, breathing lighter, it's so
unsteady
I CAN'T BREATHE!

Imperfect Woman

Imperfect together with you I'll be
The only thing that is perfect is my
imperfections
Scratches, bruises, stretch marks and scars
Packaged with unfiltered beauty
Past the eye of the beholder, deep into the mold
created for her
Filled with substance that's filtered
Using elegance clothed in ambiance
Radiance flows into existence
Exuding an aura past the surface so don't let the
flesh distract you from the purpose
Love your canvas, paint your picture
Instead of using control to protect your canvas
Love each bit of your imperfect canvas
That's the beauty of it being yours
When someone asks for the story behind it
Another facet of your creativity is allowed to
flow
I'm an imperfect woman

My But of Hearts...

My heart wants to rip, but it's not ripping
Shatter like fallen glass, into a million and one
pieces
My heart hurts, but I really don't know why....

It's been suffocated and beaten to no end.

Who wrapped my heart with concertina and
closed off the valves to keep me from breathin?
I look around for the culprit to pin, the ache in
my heart that I keep feelin,

But to my surprise, no one is there, and I
realized who I thought was there, was only a
reflection of myself...morphed into my alter
ego,

The one that is dark and wounded, unafraid to
let go...

Of the, shoulda, woulda couldas, and what if's
of life,
I have induced myself with too much strife!

My heart needs relief, its suffocating; My heart needs relief, but it's too painstaking!

The moment of release...when enough is enough,
What will I do, this road is rough!

Release seems simple and only right, but there's something about the pain that makes it feel deserved...so I won't fight

To what end will I go to torcher my heart...with unnecessary pain of thoughts running wild in my brain?!?!

Remove the concertina, but make sure you use gloves, all those holes, but yet no plugs!!

Pick up the pieces, but don't use a broom, this requires delicate hands, not a single sweep and we're through.

Reluctantly I remove the constraints from my heart, but it doesn't remove the fear because that's another part.

My fear is real and I live it every day, to not be loved for the person you see – all of that feels superficial until you really know me.

What happens then, only time will tell....

Am I willing to go another round and trust that this time it will be valued and treasured?

I guess I have to because only time WILL tell...

So here it is…my heart…torn, beaten, and bruised, ready to go another round so that bitterness will lose 🖤 🖤 💔 💔

Honest(y)(ly)

Honesty is brutal and if you're not ready

It will beat you down because your stance wasn't steady

Honestly I see you at the end of your tunnel

Allowing honesty to be your guiding angel

I'll meet you where you are even when the path is not clear

100, 200, 500, 1000

Pieces to your incomplete puzzle of life's vernacular

Resembling your beliefs intertwined by a false copula

Scattered between yesterday, today, now, forever and tomorrow

Honest because your rose tinted glasses was neither truth or reality

Just when you blink... in that moment…. life will come crashing down

Get back in the game so you can gain

Your best chance to be your best self

Not apologizing for what you left

I honestly want honesty and the honest truth is

I am your number one fan, I'm always cheering for you!

Respect the Humble in the Hustle

What makes you, you is the very thing that makes me love you

You live by your own rules, you don't conform to society's corrupt culture

You believe beauty is bold, charismatic and carefree

Being the best you is your top priority

Relationships are your foundation built on bricks of love, faith, family and friends

Even at your worst, you give your best

Your loyalty is unquestionable, your standards are always high

Your only competition is creating a better version of yourself

You're a role model that emulates the best things in life aren't things

When the world pushes, you press because
giving up will never be an option

The love I have for you comes from a place of
honor, appreciation and humility

What makes you, you is the very reason I love
you

Push and pull

When I pushed, you pulled

I pushed to fight harder
I pushed to grind deeper
I pushed my ambition into position to turn my
dreams into goals and I thought you were with
me when I pushed

So I pushed, and I pushed, then I pushed and I
turned and you were no longer beside me

You pulled
You pulled for accolades
You pulled for prestige
You pulled for everything that said I made this
team, my rules, my way I am esteemed

I pushed, you pulled

Moving towards each other but not in the same
direction

I pulled with you and lost myself so I pushed
aganist you and defined myself

Embarking on a journey to choose myself over
wealth
Choosing everyone's decisions for my life to
include you
Disappointed because over me I chose you

I thought you would be cheering by now, I mean
wouldn't you
Don't you like this gravitational pull you created
By your societal cleanup designed it
By the power vested in me no longer hiding
behind it

And now you're wondering how we ended up in
this climate

It's simple, I pushed, you pulled

I'm Fine

Hey boo
What's up gorgeous
You are beautiful..

Conversation starters with no depth or
substance,

Past the what's up and hey you's there's an
elegance
Behind chinky eyes and a beautiful smile there's
an essence

And if you blink too fast you just might miss
 The longing in her voice when distress hits

When helping others feeds her soul but leaves
her empty to bear her soul

By herself left alone with thoughts running wild.

Praying that Jesus sees her and sends her a smile
Something in the form of a hug will do.

Or the opportunity to let tears fall, and silence calls and all in all you release to no judgement just space to be raw

Even in pain you move in silence

Strong is your alias and with courage you formed an alliance

Not knowing one day you really would just for once want someone to come through and break the silence

To think of it is almost like a fairytale and just like a daydream when it looks too good to be true...

You realized the investment in you is not real so when you respond to the fifty million and one what's good, are you ok

You look through glossed eyes and a cubic zirconia smile and say...

I'm fine.

Real Eyes Realize

I know what eyes of judgement look like
Shifty, uncertain, more like unveil the curtain
Judgement is societal when being you is better
off being kept in denial
When sensitivity is more like a prenuptial need
And the seed of you won't succeed is more
potent than the seed to recede
It's caught in my throat
I hold my breath uncertain of your eyes
They tell a story that your voice would disguise
To my demise it's far from a lie
But even farther from the truth
To my surprise the eyes don't lie
I'll continue to shoot my shot to win the prize
For one day the day will come that my ambition
will match my intuition
And the message behind the eye you've been
dishing
Won't affect me like it did in the beginning
In the meantime, in between the space between
ears where I can hear your fears but your focus
is in your pupils near and dear to the portal of
your mind
Your look is loud...I can hear you.

L✶VE

Unconditionally carried
relentlessly caring
Patiently waiting
Persistently fighting
To introduce me...
To L✶VE
In spite of me, L✶VE pursued me
I tried to take it with limits, only to find its
limitless
I created boundaries for it, but it never knew
what that was
I tried to convince L✶VE it could have
conditions, but L✶VE replied that its only
provision is
uncondition
Scared....I manipulated L✶VE,
Dressed it in insecurities, drizzled in fear,
loneliness, struggles and pride
Becoming paralyzed and stagnant desperately
covering the purity of its origin

BUT NOW I KNOW DIFFERENT...

I honor L✶VE
I respect L✶VE

I magnify L✳VE

Love loved first and indescribably, I can never compete

And through L✳VE, purpose was birthed!

So now, I am ready for L✳VE

I receive you just the way you are.

Elephant

You can't see me past my circumstances
You can't hear me beyond the happenstances
I'm not what I've been through, but yet
condemnation tells you
Whisper when you see her
Pat, pat, pat her on the back when you see her
Turn your head and talk behind her back when
you see her
Have pity on her when you see her
Her truth is ugly and we don't want to deal with
her
Let's address, but rather undress her with our one
sided views and perception we"ll kill her
All this time throwing dirt on a seed
She needed roots to grow and your calloused
disposition gave her what she needed
Making her the elephant, you thought she wasn't
relevant
So in your mind you made her violent
Thinking she would run like a coward behind it
But the elephant you pushed away
She ran with vigor and found more like her
Coming back strong, the elephant stood tall
Addressing the masses she's said to all
What if I address the room?

It is me you're talking about after all
See, I know where I came from and where I've
been
According to your standards it should've
disqualified me then
According to my life it has made me the person
standing herein
Complete and total confidence, shining through
like an ambiance
ambition strong, I'm still climbing
Grinding hard I'm undeniably the best at being
me
And more importantly with me is a herd of
elephants that are just like me
Ready to trample excuses, misuses and the you
can't do its
Strong together, United we stand
In truth and favor, God will bless our hands
Walking on eggshells around me is not needed
God stands strong and perfect in my weakness
So while you're busy having pity on my past
state
I'm too bust being great
So keep on watching it's happening at an
alarming rate
I can't change your mind, but you can't change
his favor
I'm an elephant big and strong

And my time in the wilderness will prove the elephant in the room was where she needed to be all along

The Elegance of My Shoulders

From conception to fruition, He stepped out of
time to make time.
In the beginning the Word was God and the
Word was with God
In my beginning was a life full of possibilities
fledged with determination that my God is more
than enough for me to be
More than enough woman
More than enough strength to weather any storm
To dance in the rain, to shine even through the
pain.... my character speaks volumes
You can't see me if you're looking with your
eyes you can only see my true bounty if you're
looking with your heart don't mistake my trials
for weakness
God created me fearfully and wonderfully I
represent P 31. I am virtuous, competent,
magnificent, simple, courageous
Lay your head on my bosom with confidence
that you will rise up in strength
I have been fashioned by the Most High
My position has been solidified by his mercy
and grace

I am equipped to be your reward, your good
thang, your favor
Stand strong knowing....I'm built for this!

Color Me

She was a blank canvas, beautiful in simplicity
yet longing for complexity

Smooth, unblemished radiances of earth's
delight

Color me blue around my bosom because my
womb produces greatness

Color me violet around my head because I am
crowned in royalty

Color me red around my eyes because the fire in
me will always shine bright

Color me black across my feet because the steps
I take will be marked in history

Color me white across my heart because it is
pure and free from vindictiveness

Color me brown across my hands for they will
lay the foundation for which I stand

Color me bad because I will break societies rules

Color me pure for that is what my intentions will
be

Color me with your heart and spirit for there
you'll find true revelation

Color me intricate, color me bold, color me with
pages from a novel waiting to be told

With each brush stroke simplicity met
complexity and transposed purpose embedded in
possibilities

#dontwastestrokes #colormeambition
#colormemagnificent #colormestrong

Respect the Humble and the Hustle

What makes you,

you is the very thing that makes it easy to love you

You live by your own rules,

you don't conform to society's corrupt culture.

You believe beauty is bold, charismatic and carefree.

Being the best you is your top priority.

Relationships are your foundation built on bricks of love, faith, family and friends.

Even at your worst, you give your best.

Your loyalty is unquestionable,

your standards are always high.

Your only competition is creating a better version of yourself.

You're a role model that emulates the best things in life aren't things.

When the world pushes, you press because giving up will never be an option.

The love I have for you comes from a place of honor, appreciation and humility.

What makes you, you is the very reason I love you.

Winning Is Average

You're affected when life hits you
And the effect when you let it
Can be positive but be ready to be tested

Motivation runs high when you're on cloud nine
But what does it look like when you're in the
middle of the ocean and you're about to die

Sink or swim are the options they say

Sinking is for the idiot that never used their
motivation past desperation when exasperation
hit faster than a train getting to its destination

Swimming is for the average that has went
through something but the sum of the thing
didn't make you push to be better just to be
proficient

An eagle only flaps its wings a few times and
then it soars

A lion stands stills and it's presence is heard

An elephant realizes the strength in numbers so
they always move in a herd
And yet you'd rather move like the average idiot
expecting your voice to be heard

You have dominion but yet you're being
dominated
You have an opinion but instead you've negated

The fact that you are hardwired for greatness

And some where along the way

Your greatness has diminished to degrade you
and become less
Or as they say, as society has told you

Get up, show up, stand tall grow up

Excuses are excuses because you have ex'd out
of your cue to be you

And settled to do you in a less than you fashion
Being the average idiot putting the square peg in
the circle you began to ration
Your thoughts and ideas and categorized them to
be less than your passion

When does the madness end and you begin

When you realize your existence is more than
you existing to win

Embody

The reason the Bible says spare the rod
Is because it was never intended for you to use
your limbs to invoke discipline
The extension of your hand should be done in
love
Yet you've raised it in anger so in fear of you
they cower and run
An extension of grace has turned from beauty to
disgrace
The race that embodies blackness but yet still
lives in darkness
Don't release
Just give enough to appease
I'll fool you with my upstanding quotes and
hashtags "I'm living my best life"
While I embody dis-ease
The disease that's taking over like a cancer and
rotting faster than tooth decay
Cuz at the end of the day, you keep them all at
bay
Mentally tormented, jacked up relenting dealing
with the issue but really you didnt
Because there is nothing like the pain of being
stained with someone else membranes scattered

over your memories to bring to your forefront
and come at you like you're insane..

Flat Iron

This chic came at me with a flat iron
We almost had a different conversation
Can I show you something she said
Utter disgust was the look on my face that she
read
My curls define me
They represent my attitude charisma, character
and swag
I no longer a slave to straight tresses, the creamy
crack or burned edges
I no longer fear what I look like underneath
The lies and deceit sold to me in an attempt to
change my identity
My attitude is curly
My charisma kinky
My character coily
My swag is wavy
Straight is conformity like white picket fences in
cookie cut neighborhoods
I'm more like the condo 20 stories high looking
over your neighborhood
All I heard was do I want to look like you
A question barely above a challenge and just
below ambition

When selling dreams of acceptance in the form
of ceramic plates charged with heat is the
message
I'll choose to embrace my beauty unfiltered and
flawed
Before I try to dress it up in the form of your
fairytale that says I shouldn't be accepted at all
Thank you no thank you, I'll keep my curls
And the next time you try to enslave my
potential
I'll come for you like a bad influence with good
intentions
You're welcome

God make me heartless so I can live a life
detached
I asked him and he won't do it
I didn't push too hard but I had to ask
My arms are too short to try to fight let alone
test God like that
Encouraged to not be heartless as I was told
Pray for a balanced heart instead
Your story has yet to unfold
Your heart is your lifeline, a necessity needed for
your crew to soar into a life that's bold
Anything less peels back their covering if you
decide to be cold

As long as I'm breathing my children will be
under my umbrella for safe keeping
But there's no more room for the rest is left
For my tears to blend into the rain with the
unshaken truth that both are weeping to drown
out
the pain
Separate the aorta from the main muscle I say
Till the beating heart turns into a thud and there's
no more feelings left to display
Until it chooses not to scuffle but submissively
clings to being unattached, unloved, completely
muffled
Twelve rounds make a match but I think I'll tap
out early
Light a match and set on fire the idea that Boaz
will come for me
Shut down this prison less than a nightmare far
past a dream
Cascaded with frustration the train no longer
stops at this destination
Rest assured I'm not bitter just putting my
energy into other arenas
Living my best life for myself
Engulfed, indulged, satiated in me
I'm not too hard, I'm actually too soft to let
someone else fool me
Live my life as the lead role, no supporting or
extras to make this lead whole

This is a monologue for an audience of none to
take care of me the way I should've done
So instead of praying to be heartless Lord
Help me to live my best life through you so I can
live without....regardless.

Come For Me

If you gon come for me, come for me
Don't be a coward and run behind your
insecurities
Don't get yourself worked up full of hot smoke
You'll end up puffed up and roughed up by your
own words and deadly mind scuffed up
From woman I came, by God fearfully and
wonderfully made
And to think your spade in the game is your
lifeless words trying to damper something you
don't even have the power to create
Nigga please
If you gon come for me, come for me
Run real fast like you gunning for me
A turncoat I am not, but turnt up I will slot you
in your rightful place
With your jacked up mental space you have been
displaced
Careful should be the words you speak against
me
Sharper are the jewels in my crown because I'm
royalty
Over your illustrious, bodacious use of outdated
conversation...

Silence me you will not, talk to me like you own
me you cannot
Think I'm beneath you I think not
Let's solidify, I am not
Don't let me feminity confuse you into thinking
I'm automatically shook by you
So I'll say it once last time because karma's a
bitch and the third time is the charm
If you gon come for me, you betta come for me
You're a coward for even trying to run up on me
If I did 't send for you, you'll be disappointed
Your efforts are useless, you couldn't come for
me if you wanted

Petty Black Girls

I have so many knives in my back
I'm almost positive you hit a nerve and made me
a paraplegic
Machetes of hate and holding grudges
Slicing through my flesh I barely felt it go in
Couldn't even gauge how deep it went in
But I felt the fury in my blood when it oozed
down my back like venom
To think outside your petty mind and cut me
slack
A different perspective of dialogue with dignity
and tact
Your slack lacked finesse and understanding
So you upgraded to a sword
Trying to be stealth and slice me quickly
I seen you coming so I moved a little differently
Just so you couldn't bruise me permanently
We tried it your way but look where it got me
Laid out like garbage because there's no
stoppage
To your hate, abuse, misuse of power and lies
The line that was once drawn in the sand
Easily erasable by climates hand
Is now being drawn in wet cement

So when it dries the line is less remnant and
more like permanent
Which will be the same for the memories you
have of me
Etched into your mind with the simile
She's cold as ice and tough as nails
The life you're trying to make for me is the
creation of your hell

Evolved Woman

Most men aren't ready for an evolved woman..

Self sufficient, not independent because she understands her King will be THE ONE

The one who uplifts her, upholds her and with honor bestow her

To say you're ready is to admit your past, live in your present and have a vision for your future

Not to doubt where you came from but to acknowledge there is beauty in ashes and you're better because you're with her

To elevate her, celebrate her, hold her down in confidence not drama and arrogance ish

An evolved woman is an attuned woman, a kept woman, an understood woman

Her pride is beneath her, her courage before her, her presence follows her with self love paving the way for her

Don't stand in her way, she's on a mission

A vision without goals is a waste of time since there's no mission

Let her be if you're not ready to leave and cleave

Because an evolved woman has learned how to be her own lead

Only in due time and season will she leave room at her side

For a King ready to take on the evolved woman and become his Queen, strong and arrived

But until that time, daily she will evolve with stride

And ride the waves of life with dignity and a fire in her in eyes

Choosing not to concede to be less than the journey taken to evolve

Not this woman, she'll keep her resolve so men.... tread lightly.